Readers Love Denise's Playful Math Books

"Reading one of Gaskins' books is like going to a really great teacher workshop—part philosophy, part practical ideas, and all excellent. She just oozes expertise and enthusiasm."

—Amy at Hope Is the Word blog

"It revolutionized our homeschool this year."

—Caitlin Fitzpatrick Curley, My-Little-Poppies.com

"It's a crime, really, that school makes math so boring, when there are so many ways to do the opposite, for anyone who wants to. Denise Gaskins's book is full of ideas."

—Sasha Alyson, online reader review

"With this approach I can teach my kids to think like mathematicians without worrying about leaving gaps ... I can't wait to take my children by the hand and head off to explore the wonderful world of maths."

—Lucinda Leo, NavigatingByJoy.com

A PLAYFUL MATH SINGLE

Let's Play Math
SAMPLER

10 Family-Favorite Games for Learning Math Through Play

Denise Gaskins

Tabletop Academy Press

© 2019 Denise Gaskins
Print version 1.0
All rights reserved.
Except for brief quotations in critical articles or reviews, the purchaser or reader may not modify, copy, distribute, transmit, display perform, reproduce, publish, license, create derivative works from, transfer or sell any information contained in this book without the express written permission of Denise Gaskins or Tabletop Academy Press.

Tabletop Academy Press, Blue Mound, IL, USA
tabletopacademy.net

ISBN: 978-1-892083-50-0
Library of Congress Control Number: 2019900963

DISCLAIMER: This book is provided for general educational purposes. While the author has used her best efforts in preparing this book, Tabletop Academy Press makes no representation with respect to the accuracy or completeness of the contents, or about the suitability of the information contained herein for any purpose. All content is provided "as is" without warranty of any kind.

CREDITS:

Portions of this book were originally published in a different format on Denise Gaskins's Let's Play Math blog and in her playful math books for families.
DeniseGaskins.com

Cover art by photography33/DepositPhoto

"McLemore Hotel," image courtesy of the Boston Public Library/Flickr. (CC BY 2.0)
flickr.com/photos/boston_public_library/6775629674

Youth soccer photo (quote background) from USAG-Humphreys/Flickr (CC-BY-2.0)
flickr.com/photos/usaghumphreys/6206019712

Author photo by Christina Vernon:
melliru.com

Contents

The Value of Math Games 3

Let's Play Math 7
    Social Math Games 8
    The "What Number Am I?" Game 15

Counting & Number Bonds 19
    Nine Cards 21
    Snugglenumber 25

Addition & Subtraction 31
    Tiguous 33
    Chance 36

Multiplication & Fractions 39
    Times-Tac-Toe 41
    Fraction Train 44

Prealgebra & Geometry [Preview] 47
    Hit Me! 48
    The Function Machine 51

Conclusion, and What's Next? 55
    Answers to Sample Problems 59
    Quotes and Reference Links 61
    About the Author 63

Mathematics is the world's best game.

It is more absorbing than chess,
    more of a gamble than poker,
        and lasts longer than Monopoly.

It's free.

It can be played anywhere—
    Archimedes did it in a bathtub.

It is dramatic,
    challenging,
        endless,
            and full of surprises.

            —RICHARD J. TRUDEAU.

Children already know how to learn: you play around and have fun and struggle and figure it out for yourself. Grownups don't need to hold infants up and move their legs for them to teach them to walk; kids walk when there is something interesting in the room that they want to get to. So a good teacher is someone who "puts interesting things in the room," so to speak.

—Paul Lockhart

The Value of Math Games

Numbers, shapes, patterns, and puzzles—mathematics abounds with interesting things.

Children enjoy counting, and they love to think about big numbers and infinity. They delight in shapes and symmetry, and also in the sometimes-surprising balance of asymmetry.

Patterns fill our world. Geometric, repeating patterns like a fence row or tile floor. Natural, growing patterns like the branching of a tree.

As children notice and interact with the numbers, shapes, and patterns in their lives, they ask questions. Wondering is the natural mode of a child's mind—and also of a mathematician's.

Questions and puzzles, wonder and speculation, lie at the heart of mathematics. They are the "interesting things" that make our children want to learn.

Then along comes school, with its schedules and checklists.

Wonder doesn't happen on a schedule. Curiosity won't submit to checklists. We want to teach practical skills for the future, but our children only care about today.

How can we adults "put interesting things in the room" that will entice children to master these skills?

We harness the power of play.

Games Make Hard Work Fun

Math games strengthen a child's natural, intuitive understanding of numbers. And games build problem-solving skills.

Someday, addition may help our kids set up and keep a budget. Who cares? But when addition answers the important question of "Who has more?"—ah, *that* matters.

Eventually, multiplication may allow no-longer-young people to calculate their home mortgage interest or fill out an income tax form. Big whoop. But if multiplication answers the question "Did I win?"—now *that's* relevant.

Of course, understanding negative numbers will help students pass their algebra class and prepare for high school math. Boring. But what if negative numbers let them trounce their parents in a math game? *That* has intrinsic value.

Powered by the joy of play, math games push children to struggle with difficult concepts and figure them out. The ideas become their own.

While children think about their options for each turn, they puzzle through many more calculations than a typical workbook page. Yet they do it without complaining. In their concentration on the game strategy, they don't even notice how much they are learning.

Math games meet children each at their own level. The child who sits at the head of the class can solidify skills. The child who lags behind grade level can build fluency and gain confidence.

And both will learn something even more important, according to teacher and author Peggy Kaye. She writes in *Games for Math:* "If you play these games, and your child learns only that hard mental effort can be fun, you will have taught something invaluable."

Let Your Children Think

Wise teachers know that a good math lesson builds on a student's natural understanding. Children construct new math ideas on top of their own common sense notions about how the world works.

In the same way, math games let players try different strategies and approach problems in creative ways, without demanding that they use a textbook method.

If their figuring makes sense, it's fair play.

For example, suppose I need to add a chain of *integers*—positive and negative numbers—to find my score in the game Hit Me. I don't have to add the numbers in the same order I drew the cards. I can rearrange things, pairing opposites that add up to zero. Or I can add all the positive numbers together, and add all the negatives, then find the difference between those totals. Or I can work out my sum in any other way that makes sense to me.

So encourage your children to think about things their own way. You'll help them develop the flexible reasoning skills that lead to success in math.

The *Let's Play Math Sampler* features an assortment of number and logic games from my earlier book *Let's Play Math* and from the *Math You Can Play* series. Those books of playful math grew from years of experience with my own children and my homeschool co-op math classes.

As you read through this book, you'll discover that my games are never entirely about the math. I prefer games that demand reasoning, not just recall of facts. Games that require strategic interaction between the players, not just homework in disguise.

I hope your family enjoys playing these games as much as we have.

—Denise Gaskins
LetsPlayMath@gmail.com

Let's Play MATH

How Families Can Learn Math Together —and Enjoy It

DENISE GASKINS
Foreword by Keith Devlin

SAMPLE GAMES FROM

Let's Play Math

TRANSFORM YOUR CHILD'S experience of math!

Even if you struggled with mathematics in school, you can help your children enjoy learning and prepare them for academic success.

Author Denise Gaskins makes it easy with this mixture of math games, low-prep project ideas, and inspiring coffee-chat advice from a veteran mother of five.

Filled with stories and illustrations, *Let's Play Math* offers a practical, activity-filled exploration of what it means to learn math as a family.

tabletopacademy.net/lets-play-math

Social Math Games

My favorite playful math lessons rely on adult/child conversation, a proven method for increasing a child's reasoning skills.

What better way could there be to do math than snuggling up on a couch with your little one, or standing side by side at the sink while your child helps you wash the dishes, or passing the time on a car ride into town?

"If you can read with your kids, then you can talk math with them," says Christopher Danielson, author of *Talking Math with Your Kids*. "You can support and encourage their developing mathematical minds.

"You don't need to love math. You don't need to have been particularly successful in school mathematics. You just need to notice when your children are being curious about math, and you need some ideas for turning that curiosity into a conversation."[†]

Math is a social activity—asking questions, posing puzzles, noticing connections, wondering "What if...?" All these things are easier for children to do in conversation with adults.

Even the busiest families can find a few minutes here and there to talk about math. You can use everyday activities such as fixing snacks or grocery shopping to launch short chats about numbers, shapes, symmetry, or patterns.

In addition to such informal discussions, my kids and I have enjoyed social math in the form of oral story problems, mystery number puzzles, and the Today Game.

---

† *talkingmathwithkids.com*

Tell Me a Story

As soon as your children can count past five, you can start giving them simple oral story problems to solve:

> *"If you have a cookie and I give you two more cookies, how many cookies will you have then?"*

The fastest way to a young child's mind is through the taste buds. Children easily visualize their favorite foods, so I like to use edible stories at first. Then we expand our range, sharing stories about other familiar things: toys, pets, or trains.

> *"Panther the barn cat went hunting in the field. He caught two mice every day. How many mice did he catch in four days?"*

Don't limit your story problems to the child's grade level. If she can make a picture in her mind, she will be able to work with it. You may encourage your child to count on her fingers: one finger for each mouse. Using fingers as symbols is a step into abstraction, paving the way for later algebra.

If you dislike finger-counting, then show your children how to use blocks or a hundred chart to work with bigger numbers than they can handle on their own. You can find a bunch of ideas for playing math with a hundred chart on my blog.†

> *"Panther went out to the woods and met a gray cat named Shadow. He invited her to come back to our barn and chase pigeons. There were fifteen pigeons in the barn. Panther chased six of them. He let Shadow have the rest. How many pigeons did Shadow chase?"*

As you both get used to the game, you can occasionally throw in something harder, such as fractions, division with a remainder, or an answer that comes out negative. See what your child can do with a tough problem. You might be surprised: even a toddler has ideas about how to split three hot dogs between two people.

---

† denisegaskins.com/2008/09/22/things-to-do-hundred-chart

If your children are stumped, try not to give away the answer. Instead, ask them to explain the problem back to you. As children put a problem into their own words, they often see how to approach the solution. Pretend to be Socrates, asking questions to guide their thinking.

> "After Shadow came to live in the barn, we had two cats, and half of them were girls. But then Shadow had four kittens. Now two-thirds of our barn cats are girls. How many of the kittens were girl cats?"

Here is the most important rule of the oral story problem game: take turns. If I ask my daughter a story problem, she gets to give me one. And I have to try to solve it, even if she uses made-up numbers such as eighty-hundred or a gazillion. This is playtime, not an oral quiz.

Things to Consider in Creating Story Problems

- Some quantities are discrete and countable, such as marbles or dinosaurs. Other quantities are continuous, such as a pitcher of juice or a length of rope. We want our children to feel comfortable working with problems of both types.

- We often think of addition and subtraction as putting together or taking away sets of discrete items. But they can also be represented in stories by growth or comparison (how much more or less) or by classification (some are female cats and some are male).

- We often think of multiplication and division as counting or splitting up groups of items. But we can also think of these math processes as growth or shrinkage (how many times as much) or as rates and ratios (cookies per child, hot dogs per package).

- Division of continuous quantities may lead naturally to fractions (sharing pizza or candy bars).

Equal sharing leads to fractions. Can you see how to divide this candy bar into halves, thirds, fourths, sixths, or twelfths?

- Money provides an excellent way for children to begin playing with decimal numbers.

If you have trouble coming up with stories, you can still make oral story problems a part of your routine by reading the blog Bedtime Math. Laura Overdeck posts a daily math story (with answers) at three levels of difficulty, preschool to middle-elementary.[†]

Oral story problems are not just for young children. Students of all ages benefit from the practice of working math in their heads. As your children grow, let the stories grow with them: soccer games, horse stories, or space adventures will keep older students figuring.

For more tips on creating and solving story problems, check out my book *Word Problems from Literature*.

Can You Guess My Secret?

As they reach school age, children are ready to try a more abstract challenge. This doesn't mean you should stop playing with stories, but it's a good time to add another social math game to your repertoire. Now you can introduce the idea of *variables*, or unknown mystery numbers.

---

† *bedtimemath.org*

First grade algebra on a whiteboard. She solved my problems, and then she wrote problems for me to solve. Like all artists, we signed our work.

Elementary textbooks slip a few pages of stealth algebra into even the earliest years with "missing addend" problems, which look like this:

$$5 + \_\_ = 7.$$

Encourage your children to do mystery number problems, both orally and written out. My children love to do math with colored markers on a whiteboard. You can use a question mark or an empty square to stand for the secret number.

And you can sometimes use a letter symbol, to ease your children's transition to algebra: "I know a mystery number. I can't tell you its name, so I'll call it N. If you had N plus thirteen more, that would be twenty-five."

$$N + 13 = 25$$

"Can you tell what my number is?"

Don't forget to take turns. When you let the kids make up problems for you, math remains a game. Children love trying to outwit adults.

The Today Game

If you pay attention to the everyday numbers around you, you will see plenty of opportunities to play with mental math. Try posting a small whiteboard on the front of your refrigerator with "Today is [Month] [Date]" written across the top. Throughout the day, family members can write different creative names for the date.

For instance, I am typing this on November 14, so we might invent such names as:

$$1 + 2 + 3 + 2 + 1 + 2 + 3$$
$$4 \times 7 \div 2$$
$$20 - (10 - 4)$$
$$56 \times 1/4$$
$$84 - 70$$

Or watch the display on your digital clock. How many number expressions or math equations can you make with the time?

8:24 makes 8 = 2 × 4
10:43 makes 1 + 0 = 4 − 3
1:03 is the prime number 103 = prime time

Keep a chart, and let family members add a sticker for each "clock math" expression they find. Whoever wins the most stickers is proclaimed the family's Clock Math Champion.

The "What Number Am I?" Game

WRITING FOR *FAMILY Life* magazine, mathematician and music critic Edward Rothstein described a game he invented for his daughter:

"What number am I? If you add me to myself, you get four."

I gave that question to my six-year-old daughter during a family car trip. Then her sister, age nine, wanted to play. I tried a question with bigger numbers, but she rolled her eyes. "That's too easy, Mom."

So I asked her:

"What number am I? If you take away one-fourth of me and then add two, you get seventeen."

Hint: You can find the answers to these sample problems in the appendix. This problem has two possible solutions, depending on how you understand the words in the question. My daughter did not see it the same way I did. Her answer caught me by surprise — it was three times the number I expected — and yet after she explained her reasoning, I had to admit that her solution, too, was correct.

Let this be a warning: if your child's answer is not the same as yours, don't assume she is wrong. Ask her to explain how she figured it out. Then listen with care. Children almost always have a logical reason for their answers. Language is a complicated thing, and even a math problem may be open to different interpretations.

The older our children get, the harder their parents have to work. For my twelve-year-old son, I asked:

"What number am I? If you multiply me by myself and add one, you get half as many as the number of pennies in a dollar."

That kept him busy for a few minutes. After he figured it out, he came back with:

"What number am I? If you divide me by two and take away four, then add five, then multiply by three and divide by two and add seven, you get me again."

"What?" I asked.

He repeated the question.

"This is actually a number?" I asked. "You figured out an answer to this?"

He nodded, with the smug grin of a preteen who knows he has Mom skewered.

I pulled out a notebook and pen. He repeated his series of calculations, and this time I wrote it down. I figured the answer had to be zero or one, those magic numbers that make multiplying easy, but neither worked.

I tried one hundred. No luck.

I heard a chuckle from the back seat.

"Wait," I said. "Give me a chance."

My husband was driving, but he glanced over at the notebook. "You know," he offered, "you could set that up as an equation."

No way. The boy had not needed algebra to figure it out, so neither did I. Still guessing, I tried ten, then fifty, then twenty. OK, that narrowed it down. Now I knew the answer had to be between twenty and fifty, but I had run out of easy numbers.

I nibbled on the end of my pen.

My son hummed to himself.

"I've got it." I spun around as far as the seat belt allowed. "The answer is—"

"Nope."

"What?!"

I looked at my scratch paper. I worked the numbers again, coming up with the same answer. I read the steps of my calculation out loud.

He agreed that my number would work, but it was not the one he had in mind. I would have to guess again.

Hubby protested that there couldn't be another answer. If the equation doesn't have an x^2 or something similar, there can't be more than one solution.

The kid stood his ground, smirking.

I conceded. "What's your number?"

"Infinity. It doesn't matter what you multiply or take away, it's always infinity."

Aha! He was right. Well, sort of right: infinity isn't a real number, so you can't calculate with it that way. But it's good enough for middle school.

Even better, he had managed to stump the adults.

The topic of infinity captures a child's imagination and
may lead to a lifelong fascination with math.
In the 1920s, mathematician David Hilbert created a story about
an imaginary grand hotel with an infinite number of rooms.
hotel-infinity.com

Math You Can Play

Grades **PK-2**

Counting & Number Bonds

Math Games for Early Learners

DENISE GASKINS

SAMPLE GAMES FROM

Counting & Number Bonds

PREPARE YOUR CHILD for math success—by playing games!

You'll love these math games because they give your child a sturdy foundation for understanding mathematics. Young children play with counting and number recognition. Older students explore place value, build number sense, and begin learning the basics of addition.

Counting & Number Bonds features 21 kid-tested games, offering a variety of challenges for preschool and early-elementary learners.

tabletopacademy.net/math-you-can-play/#counting

Number Game Printables Pack

This pack includes:
- Assorted graph paper
- 1–100 and 0–99 charts
- Shut the Box cut-and-fold
- Game boards and score sheets

You can download a 23-page PDF file of graph paper and printable game boards at *tabletopacademy.net/free-printables*.

Nine Cards

MATH CONCEPTS: addition, number bonds for ten.
PLAYERS: two or more.
EQUIPMENT: one deck of math cards.

How to Play

The first player shuffles the deck and then turns up the top nine cards, placing them face up in a 3 × 3 array: three rows with three cards in each row. The player captures (removes and keeps) any tens and any pairs of cards that sum to ten, then passes the deck to the next player.

Each player in turn deals out enough cards to fill in the empty spots in the array—or, if there are no empty spots to fill, the player covers all nine cards with new ones. Then capture any tens and any pairs that make ten, and pass the deck on.

The game ends when the deck is gone or when there are not enough cards left to fill in the holes in the array. Whoever has collected the most cards wins the game.

Variation

CONCENTRATION (MEMORY): Lay all the cards out face down on the table in a single layer with no overlaps. On your turn, flip up two cards. If you find a ten or a number bond, take it. If not, leave the cards showing long enough that all the players can see what they are. Then turn them face down before the next player's turn.

History

Tens Concentration has always been one of my favorite number bond games. A *number bond* is a pair of numbers that sum to a given target. Thinking about number bonds prepares children for mental math because it helps them realize there are many ways to make any number.

The face-up Nine Cards version comes from Constance Kamii's *Young Children Continue to Reinvent Arithmetic*.

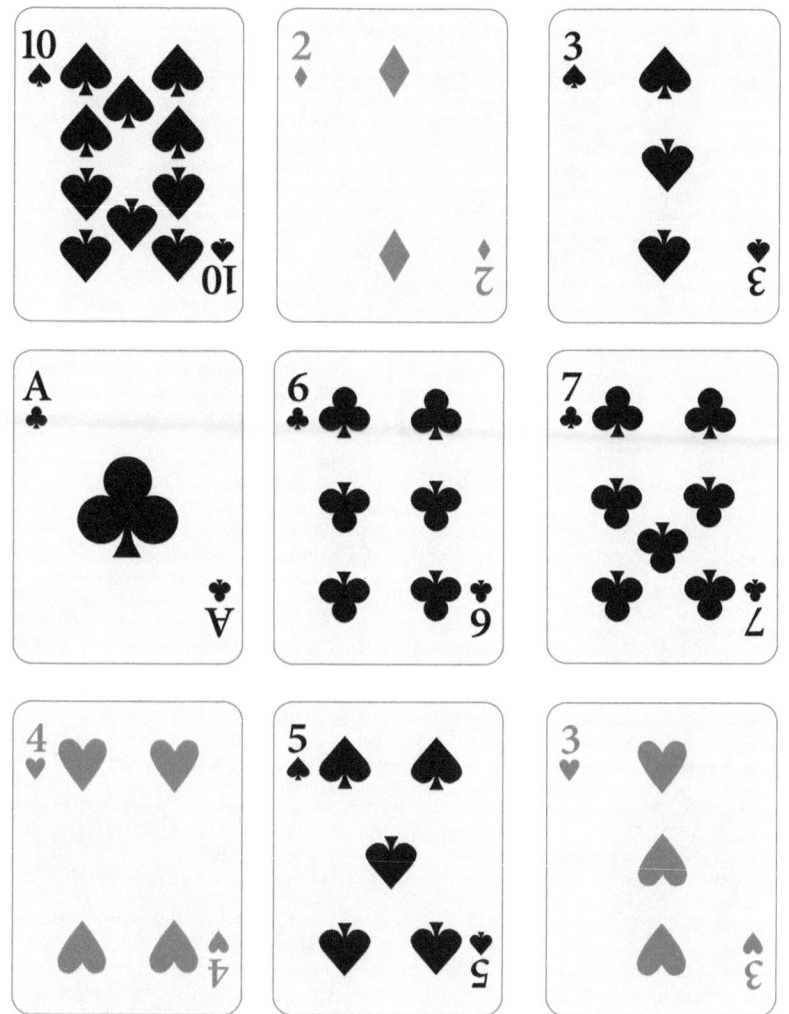

Claim the ten and the pairs of cards that add up to ten. Do not take longer sums, like 5 + 2 + 3.

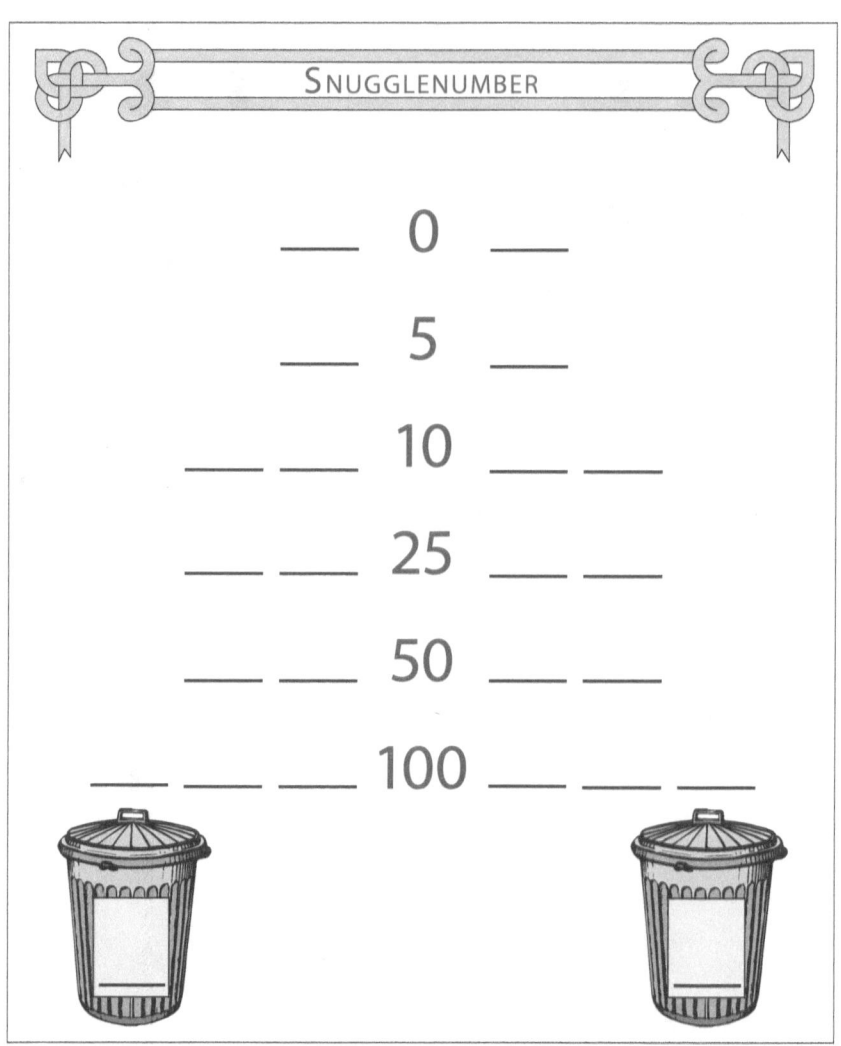

The Snugglenumber game board is included in the *Number Game Printables Pack,* but it's easy to make your own.

Snugglenumber

MATH CONCEPTS: place value, probability, thinking ahead.
PLAYERS: any number.
EQUIPMENT: one deck of math cards, pens or pencils, blank paper or free printable game boards.

Set-Up

You can print the Snugglenumber game board from the *Number Game Printables Pack* or have your children make their own game board.[†]

To make your own game boards, write the numbers 0, 5, 10, 25, 50, 100 down the center of your paper. These are the *snugglenumbers* (target numbers). Next to each number, draw as many blanks as there are digits in the target number. These blanks are where you do your snuggling. The printable sheet has two columns of blanks, which can be used for two separate games. Or two players may share one game board, each using one of the columns.

Remove the tens from your deck of cards and replace them with queens to represent the number zero — or leave in the tens, but count them as zeros. Shuffle the deck and place it in the center of the table where everyone can reach.

How to Play

On your turn, flip one card face up beside the deck. Each player must write that number on one of their blanks, trying to create numbers in

---

[†] tabletopacademy.net/free-printables

Snugglenumber game in progress. If the next card is a six, where would you put it?

each row that are as close to the snugglenumbers as possible. The next player waits until everyone has filled a blank before turning up the next card.

Once you have written a digit, it cannot be moved. But the printable game board includes a trash can symbol, so once in each game you can decide to throw away a card, writing its number value in the can instead of on a blank.

When all the blanks are filled in, players compare their numbers. Whoever has the snuggliest number in each row gets a point. In the case of a tie — either the players made the same number, or they made two numbers that are equally close to the target — both players earn a point. Whoever wins the most points wins the game.

A Sample Game

Sven challenged Olaf to a game of Snugglenumber. Olaf drew first, turning up an ace. Both players wrote a one on their game board. Olaf put his by the zero. Since one is very close to zero, he thought he had a good chance of winning that row. Sven wrote his one in the hundreds place.

Then Sven turned up a four, so both players found a place for that digit. Sven wrote his four next to the five — only one point away, a likely winner. Olaf put his four in the tens place next to the fifty, figuring a large number was bound to come along for the ones place.

Olaf's turn to draw, and he got an eight. He wrote it next to the four, making forty-eight and snuggling very close to the fifty. Sven put the eight in the twenty-five row, hoping to draw a two later in the game.

Sven turned up a six, and the players wrote it in. Then Olaf turned up a queen, which stands for a zero. Sven pounced on the chance to score on the zero row. Olaf put his zero in the hundreds place, hoping to draw nines later. Then Sven turned up another zero…

Variations

For older students, the players subtract the numbers they made from the snugglenumbers — or vice versa, depending on which is bigger — and then add up all these differences. The player with the smallest total difference wins.

HORSESHOES: Using a math card deck with zeros (queens or tens, as above), deal eleven cards to each player. Arrange your cards in the snuggle-chart pattern so that the number on each line comes as close to the target number as you can get it. Score according to horseshoe rules:

- ♦ 3 points for each *ringer*, or exact hit on the target.
- ♦ 1 point for each number that is six or less away from the target.
- ♦ If none of the players land in the scoring range for one of the target numbers, then score 1 point for the number closest to that target.

For a quick game, whoever scores the most points wins. Or follow tradition and keep going until one player gets 21 points, or 40 points for a championship game. In traditional horseshoes, you have to win by at least 2 points over your closest opponent's score.

History

I first saw place value games on the late-1980s PBS *Square One Television* series, which had a faux game show routine called "But Who's Counting?" Math teacher Anna Weltman posted this version at her blog Recipes for π.

"The game of Snugglenumber has taken my school by storm," Weltman writes. "Kids from third grade to tenth-grade Algebra 2 beg to play it. It involves the seemingly mundane arithmetic concept of place value. And yet, everyone loves it.

"Oh, and did I mention that when you say Snugglenumber you *must* scrunch up your nose, smile adorably, and coo, 'Snug-gle-num-ber'?"†

† recipesforpi.wordpress.com/2013/10/16/snugglenumber

Math You Can Play Grades K-4

Addition & Subtraction
Math Games for Elementary Students

DENISE GASKINS

SAMPLE GAMES FROM

Addition & Subtraction

PREVENT MATH ANXIETY—by playing games!

Help your child learn mental flexibility by playing with numbers, from basic math facts to the hundreds and thousands. Logic games build strategic thinking skills, and dice games give students hands-on experience with probability.

Addition & Subtraction features 23 kid-tested games, offering a variety of challenges for elementary-age students.

tabletopacademy.net/math-you-can-play/#addition

Add or subtract the numbers on your dice to make an answer that matches any unmarked square on the board. Try to touch as many previously marked squares as possible

Tiguous

MATH CONCEPTS: addition, subtraction, multistep calculation.
PLAYERS: two or more.
EQUIPMENT: free printable game board, three six-sided dice, pencil or marker(s), scratch paper for keeping score.

Set-Up

You can print the Tiguous game board from the *Number Game Printables Pack*, download the Contig, Jr. game from Terry Kawas's MathWire website, or have your children make their own game board.[†]

If students make their own board, they can arrange the numbers however they like:

- Draw a 6 × 6 grid of squares, each big enough for a two-digit number.
- The first player writes the number one in any square. The next chooses a square for the number two. Players take turns writing the numbers 1–18 anywhere they wish, one number per square.
- After eighteen, the next player goes back to one, and the turns continue until the board is full.

---

†   *tabletopacademy.net/free-printables*
mathwire.com/games/contigjr.pdf

How to Play

On your turn, roll all three dice. If any die falls off the table or lands at a slant, all three dice must be rolled again. Do not touch the dice with your hands after they are rolled, though you may use a pencil or marker to scoot them next to each other.

Add or subtract these three numbers in a two-step equation that equals the number in any unmarked square on the game board. Think of as many possible combinations as you can, in order to choose the highest-scoring square. Mark your answer on the game board with a large X. At the same time, say out loud how you calculated the number.

You score 1 point for the square you marked, plus 1 point for each already-marked square that is touching (*contiguous* to) any side or corner of your number's square. The maximum score for any turn is 9 points. If all the numbers you can make have already been marked, you score a zero—but if anyone else can find a valid calculation using your dice, that player may challenge you, mark the square, and "steal" those points.

If another player thinks you made an arithmetic mistake, that person may challenge your answer before the next player rolls the dice. If your answer was wrong, the challenger takes the points you would have won, and you score zero. If your calculation is correct, you get one bonus point for having withstood the challenge.

Play until each player has had ten turns, or five turns each for three or more players. Whoever has the highest total score wins the game.

Variations

The most common variation I have seen is not to score a point for the marked square. Just score 1 point for each contiguous square that was previously marked, which makes the maximum possible score per turn only 8 points. I strongly prefer the scoring system above, which awards at least 1 point for any valid calculation.

TIGUOUS-TAC-TOE: Two players mark numbers with X and O, and the first player to get three squares in a row wins. Rows may be vertical, horizontal, or diagonal. For a longer game, try to get four or five in a row.

MULTIPLAYER EXTENDED GAME: Keep playing until almost all the numbers are marked. Any player who gets a zero three turns in a row drops out of the game. When the last player gets a third strike, the game is over. There is no bonus for the last player, other than the extra turn(s).

TOURNAMENT RULES: Two players per game board. Set a timer, giving each player only thirty seconds for each turn. Think fast! If you do not mark a square within the thirty seconds, your score is zero for that turn. Scores of zero may not be challenged in tournament play, but opponents may challenge arithmetic errors.

After each player has ten turns, add up the players' scores for that round. Then trade partners, get a new game board, and play another round. After three rounds, award 1st, 2nd, and 3rd place ribbons to the top scorers in each age group/grade level.

History

Tiguous is a simplified version of F. W. Broadbent's game Contig, which is played on a larger board and allows the use of multiplication and division. I took the name from an even simpler version by Constance Kamii.

For as long as I can remember, our local homeschool group has held a series of Contig practices every spring. Then we host a "school" tournament, and the top two players in each grade level proceed to a regional tournament against other public and private school teams.

Chance

MATH CONCEPTS: addition beyond one hundred, probability with dice.
PLAYERS: two or more.
EQUIPMENT: five six-sided dice, paper and pencil for keeping score.

How to Play

On your turn, roll all of the dice. Set aside the numbers you would like to keep, and roll the rest of the dice again. If you wish, you may roll once more. After the third roll, add up all the numbers on the dice, and then add that sum to your game score. Pass the dice to the next player. Whoever is the first to reach or pass 300 points wins the game.

Variations

If you don't have five dice, you can still play, but you'll probably want to set a lower target number.

COUNTDOWN: Start at three hundred and subtract the numbers you roll.

PIG: In the mood for some risk? Using one or two dice, roll as many times as you wish, mentally adding each roll to keep a running total for that turn. You may stop whenever you want and add the total to your score, or keep rolling to collect more points. But if on any roll, either die shows a one, you get zero points for that turn. The two-dice variation has an additional danger: if both dice come up one, all the points you have saved so far disappear, and your game score goes back to zero.

The first player to reach or pass 100 points wins the game.

History

Dice games are easy to modify for practicing all sorts of math. Keep a pair of dice in your pocket or bag, and you will always have a way to entertain children (or yourself) in a restaurant or waiting room.

Chance is a much-simplified version of the commercial game Yahtzee. Pig is a folk-game cousin to Farkle and was first described in print by American magician and author John Scarne in his 1945 book *Scarne on Dice*.

Math You Can Play — Grades 2-6

Multiplication & Fractions
Math Games for Tough Topics

DENISE GASKINS

SAMPLE GAMES FROM

Multiplication & Fractions

RESCUE YOUR CHILD from math phobia — by playing games!

You'll love these math games because they give your child a sturdy foundation for understanding multiplication and fractions.

Help your child master the times tables and build mental math skills. Play with advanced concepts such as division, fractions, decimals, and multi-step calculations.

Multiplication & Fractions features 25 kid-tested games, offering a variety of challenges for upper-elementary and middle school students.

tabletopacademy.net/math-you-can-play/#multfrac

MULTIPLICATION & FRACTION PRINTABLES

This pack includes:

- Multiplication Models card deck
- Fraction Models card deck
- Times Tables, choose 10 × 10 or 12 × 12
- Assorted graph paper
- 1–100 and 0–99 charts
- And other game boards for playing with multiplication, fraction, and decimal math

The 44-page PDF *Multiplication & Fraction Printables* file includes blank times tables for practicing math facts up to 10 × 10 or 12 × 12.
tabletopacademy.net/free-printables

Times-Tac-Toe

MATH CONCEPTS: multiplication facts, times tables.
PLAYERS: best with two.
EQUIPMENT: printed blank times-table chart, deck of math cards, colored markers or a set of matching tokens for each player.

How to Play

Label the top row and left column of your blank times-table chart with the numbers 1–10, in numerical order or mixed around.

On your turn, flip two cards. Multiply them and find the corresponding square on the times table. If that square is blank, write in the product with your colored marker. Or say the product aloud while you cover that square with one of your tokens. If a player writes or says the wrong answer, the other player may challenge, give the correct product, and then take that square.

Sometimes you will have a choice of two squares, but you may mark only one of them. On the other hand, if there are no remaining spaces for your product, then you lose that turn. The first player to mark four squares touching (with no gaps) in a row—horizontally, vertically, or diagonally—wins the game.

Variations

For a longer game, play until someone marks five squares in a row.

If you prefer teaching the multiplication facts up to 12 × 12, you can include face cards in your deck: jack = 11, queen = 12, and king

×									

With blank labels on the top and side of the chart, players are not limited to the basic single-digit multiplication facts. Try scrambling the rows and columns and using greater numbers for added challenge.

= wild card. A player who turns up a king may use any number in its place.

TIMES TABLE GOMOKU: No math cards. Players may choose any unclaimed square and write in the product of the row and column numbers. For a tougher challenge, one player fills the top row with any numbers greater than five, and the other player chooses similar numbers for the left-column squares. As in traditional Gomoku, it takes five in a row to win.

HUNDRED-TAC-TOE: Instead of a times-table chart, use a printed 100 chart. On your turn, flip one card, and you may mark any multiple of that number which has not already been taken. Say the factors of your multiple: if you draw a two, and you want to mark forty-six, say, "Two times twenty-three." Whenever you get four (or more) squares in a row, mark them with a solid line. Go through the whole deck, and the player who marks the most lines wins.

History

People all around the world have played make-a-row games since ancient times, with a wide assortment of rules. Claudia Zaslavsky surveys the history of such games in *Tic Tac Toe and Other Three-in-a-Row Games from Ancient Egypt to the Modern Computer*.

Fraction Train

MATH CONCEPTS: proper and improper fractions, comparing and ordering fractions.
PLAYERS: any number.
EQUIPMENT: one set of double-six or double-nine dominoes.

How to Play

Remove the double-blank tile. Turn all remaining domino tiles face down on the table and mix them around to make the wood pile. Each player draws six tiles from the wood pile but *does not look at them*. Players arrange their tiles in a row (train) of fractions, as shown. When all players are ready, turn the tiles in your train face up without changing which side of the tiles is at the top of each fraction.

Your goal is to make your fraction train increase from left to right, but of course it will be mixed up to start with. On your turn, draw one tile and turn it to create a *proper fraction* (numerator less than denominator) or *improper fraction* (numerator equal to or greater than denominator) with the numbers on the two halves of the domino.

You have three choices:

- Use the new fraction to replace one of the domino tiles in your train. Then discard the old one, mixing it into the wood pile.
- If you don't want to use the new fraction, put it back and mix up the tiles.
- *Instead of drawing a new tile,* you may use your turn to

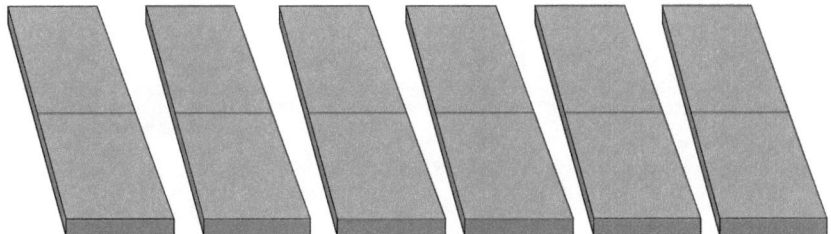

A domino number train, ready to flip and play.

rotate one of your current tiles, inverting the numerator and denominator of that fraction.

The first player to complete a train of fractions that increases from left to right wins the game.

Variations

Play with a different number of tiles. Try a shorter train for a quick game, or longer for a greater challenge.

House Rule: Decide how strict you will be about the "increases from left to right" rule and repeated numbers. Will you consider equivalent fractions as part of a valid train? Or will the player have to keep trying for a domino to replace one of the equivalents?

Math Models Number Train: Play with either the multiplication or fraction deck of math model cards in the *Multiplication & Fraction Printables* file. With the multiplication cards, the value of the products must increase from left to right.[†]

History

Fraction Train has been a favorite game in my middle school math club for years. We began by playing the game with Fraction Bars, but dominoes are cheaper and offer more variety.

[†] *tabletopacademy.net/free-printables*

Math You Can Play — Grades 4-9

Prealgebra & Geometry
Math Games for Middle School

DENISE GASKINS

Sample Games from

Prealgebra & Geometry [Preview]

Help your children learn to think mathematically.

A true understanding of mathematics requires more than the ability to memorize procedures.

Prepare your child for high school math by playing with positive and negative integers, number properties, mixed operations, functions, and coordinate geometry.

Coming soon from Tabletop Academy Press.

Hit Me!

MATH CONCEPTS: addition, subtraction, negative numbers, absolute value.
PLAYERS: two or more.
EQUIPMENT: one deck of math cards (two decks may be needed for a large group).

How to Play

Deal one card face down for each player, and then turn one card face up beside each face down card. Players do not pick up their cards! Each player may peek at his own face down card as often as he likes, but it remains hidden from the other players until the end of the round. The card that is face up remains visible to all players.

Each player mentally calculates the sum of the numbers on his cards. Aces count as one. Black cards (positive numbers) are added to the total; red cards (negative numbers) are subtracted. A player's score may go below zero.

When all players have had a chance to check their cards, the dealer asks each in turn whether he wants a *hit*—an extra card, also dealt face up so everyone can see it. If the player wants the extra card, he says, "Hit me!" Last of all, the dealer may take a hit, if he wishes.

Then each player in turn has a chance to ask for a second hit, and so forth. Players may take up to five hits, for a maximum of seven cards, or they may *hold* (stick with the cards they already have) at any time. The round is over when all the players have either taken their maximum number of hits or refused any more cards. At the end of the round, each player turns his hidden card face up and announces his score.

The player with the lowest absolute value (the sum closest to zero, whether positive or negative) wins the round. When every player has had a chance to deal, whoever has won the most rounds is the champion.

Variations

Allow the aces to count as one or eleven, player's choice.

Rather than bothering to keep score, we let the winner of each round deal the next one. If there is a tie, then whoever has not dealt recently gets a chance. Or keep a running total of each player's scores. After everyone has dealt, the player who has the lowest total absolute value is the winner.

History

The all-time favorite math game at our house, Hit Me is a variation on the traditional gambling game Blackjack, in which players aim for a total of twenty-one. I originally called the game Zero, but my boys refused to acknowledge such a boring name.

I am often surprised at the score it takes to win a hand of Hit Me. If I have a sum of three or more, I will almost always lose unless I take another card. If I take the maximum number of hits, however, that is a sign of desperation. I remember one game when all the red cards came my way, for a total of −37, as I kept trying without luck for at least one black number—and my math students were laughing and cheering at every hit I took.

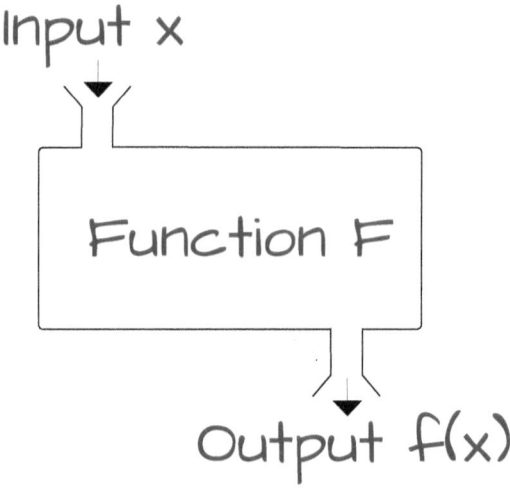

In math, a *function* is any rule that will take an input number and match it with a specific output.

[Below] An input/output chart, ready to play.

Input	Output

The Function Machine

MATH CONCEPTS: addition, subtraction, multiplication, division, fractions, odd numbers, even numbers, negative numbers, absolute value, rounding off, prime numbers, square numbers, problem solving.
PLAYERS: two or more.
EQUIPMENT: pencil and paper for keeping track of input/output numbers.

Set Up

Players each need their own pencil and paper. One person plays the role of the Function Machine, making up a rule for calculating with whatever numbers the other players provide. Here is an example of a function rule:

Double the number, and then add seven.

The Function Machine should write the function rule on a piece of paper and slip it in a pocket for reference as needed. All the other players make themselves an input/output chart to keep track of the game.

How to Play

Each player in turn says a number that hasn't yet been used, and all players write that number in their Input columns. The Function Machine calculates with that number—mentally or on scratch paper, *but not aloud*—and says the matching answer. All players write that number in their Output columns.

If the input number is too difficult, the Function Machine may say, "That's too hard," and ask for a different number.

Occasionally, players will give an input number that does not make sense with the chosen rule. The Function Machine can say "That does not compute" or "That number in not in my function's domain." The *domain* of a function is the set of allowable input numbers, and the *range* is the set of potential outputs.

If you think you know the function rule, you must wait for your turn. When you give your input number, say, "I predict the output will be _____." If the Function Machine confirms your prediction, then you're allowed to guess the function rule.

The first player to correctly identify the function rule wins that round and becomes the new Function Machine.

Variation

If you want to guess the rule, you must first give the correct output for any challenge number the Function Machine proposes.

Tip: Prepare Rules in Advance

My co-op math students have always enjoyed this game, especially when it is their turn to know the secret rule.

But some kids freeze mentally at the task of creating a function rule, while others make up rules that are so complex they are nearly impossible to guess.

So I make a list of suggested function rules in advance, writing the rules on index cards and letting each player draw a rule from the deck. Usually, I tell them to draw three cards and choose their favorite.

Here are some Function Machine rules we have used:

- Add 15 to the number.
- Subtract 4 from the number.

- Multiply the number by 8.
- Cut the number in half.
- Cut the number in half, and then add one.
- Double the number, and then subtract three.
- Add the next larger number, so an input of 3 matches an output of 3 + 4 = 7.
- Multiply by the next larger number, so an input of 5 gives an output of 5 × 6 = 30.
- Triple the next larger number.
- Subtract the number from 25.
- Square the number, and then add one.
- Say the largest multiple of 3 that is less than the number.
- Round off to the nearest hundred.
- Double the odd numbers, but cut the even numbers in half.
- All odd numbers match an output of 17, but all even numbers match 12.
- Say the ones digit of the number.
- Add the digits in the number together.
- If the number is prime, say the number. If the number is not prime, say 1. (Remember that one, zero, fractions, and negative numbers are not prime.)
- Say the tenths digit of the number (the first digit after the decimal place). The student may need a calculator to rapidly convert fractions to decimal numbers.

Comments

This is a great game to play in the car on family trips, since there are no little game pieces and the paper does not need to be passed around.

Beware that some function rules can be described in more than one way. For example, the rule:

Double the number, and then add two.

...could also be written as:

Double the next higher number.

If you are playing with younger students, it helps to have a referee who knows algebra to judge the guesses. "Double the number, and then add two" is written as $2x + 2$, while "double the next higher number" is $2(x + 1)$. Anyone who knows algebra can easily see these are the same.

The player who tries to guess the rule does not have to put it in the exact words the Function Machine used, as long as the statements are equivalent.

I would like to win over those who consider mathematics useful, but colourless and dry — a necessary evil. No other field can offer, to such an extent as mathematics, the joy of discovery, which is perhaps the greatest human joy.
— Rózsa Péter

Conclusion, and What's Next?

Math is not just rules and rote memory. Math is like ice cream, with more flavors than you can imagine.

If your child's only experience of math was in a school textbook, that would be like eating broccoli-flavored ice cream. But once your children have tasted the delicious variety of playful math, they'll never want to be limited to the school-flavored stuff.

And they don't have to be. Your whole family can feast on the wonderful abundance that is mathematics.

So where do you go from here?

- ♦ If you want more math games, I've posted several for free on my blog.[†]
- ♦ You can find more mathematical adventures through my internet resource lists.[‡]
- ♦ And explore the wonderful world of living books for math.[§]

[†] denisegaskins.com/2017/01/07/my-favorite-math-games
[‡] denisegaskins.com/internet-math-resources
[§] denisegaskins.com/living-math-books

Finally, if you've enjoyed the math games in this sampler, I hope you'll consider investing in one or more of my full-length playful math books.

…and may the Math be with you!

Answers to Sample Problems

[1] After Shadow came

We had two cats, and then four kittens, so now we have a total of six cats. Two-thirds of them are girl cats, which means we have four girl cats. One of these is the mother, Shadow, so the other three are girl kittens.

[2] If you take away one-fourth

The answer is twenty or sixty, depending on how you interpreted the question. When you "take away one-fourth," are you taking that portion as your share, or are you subtracting it and keeping the other three-fourths?

If you think of "take away" as subtraction, as if you are throwing that portion away, then you get my answer:

$$(1 - 1/4) N + 2 = 17$$
$$3/4 \times N = 15$$
$$N = 20$$

If you take the portion as your share, like taking a large piece of pizza, you will find my daughter's answer:

$$1/4 \times N + 2 = 17$$
$$1/4 \times N = 15$$
$$N = 60$$

[3] If you multiply me by myself

Work backward. There are 100 pennies in a dollar, so half that would be fifty. Then subtract the one that was added, which gives forty-nine. The secret number times itself must equal forty-nine, so that means the number is seven.

[4] If you divide me by two

To write the whole mess in algebra:

$$(\{[(x \div 2) - 4 + 5] \times 3\} \div 2) + 7 = x$$

I solved it by guessing numbers until I found one that worked, but you could use algebra to save time. Simplify the brackets from the inside out:

$$(\{[(x/2) + 1] \times 3\} \div 2) + 7 = x$$
$$(\{[3x/2] + 3\} \div 2) + 7 = x$$
$$(\{3x/4\} + 1.5) + 7 = x$$
$$(3x/4) + 8.5 = x$$
$$8.5 = x/4$$
$$8.5 \times 4 = x = 34$$

Quotes and Reference Links

ALL THE WEBSITE LINKS IN this book were checked before publication, but the Internet is volatile. If a website disappears, you can run a browser search for the author's name or article title. Or try entering the web address at the Internet Archive Wayback Machine.
archive.org/web/web.php

BROADBENT, F. W. "Contig: A Game to Practice and Sharpen Skills and Facts in the Four Fundamental Operations," *The Arithmetic Teacher*, May 1972.
jstor.org/stable/41188047
Or download the tournament Rules (PDF):
maconpiattroe.org/vimages/shared/vnews/stories/54c95745dbc67/Contig%20Rules.pdf

BROWN, TOVA. "Hotel Infinity: Parts 1–5," Hotel Infinity website, 2014.
hotel-infinity.com

DANIELSON, CHRISTOPHER. "If you can read with your kids…" from *Talking Math with Your Kids*, self-published, 2013.
talkingmathwithkids.com

GASKINS, DENISE. "30+ Things to Do with a Hundred Chart," Let's Play Math blog, September 22, 2008.
denisegaskins.com/2008/09/22/things-to-do-hundred-chart

KAMII, CONSTANCE, WITH LESLIE BAKER HOUSMAN. *Young Children Reinvent Arithmetic: Implications of Piaget's Theory*, 2nd ed., Teachers College Press, 2000.

— WITH LINDA LESLIE JOSEPH. *Young Children Continue to Reinvent Arithmetic, 2nd Grade: Implications of Piaget's Theory*, 2nd ed., Teachers College Press, 2004.

— WITH SALLY JONES LIVINGSTON. *Young Children Continue to Reinvent Arithmetic, 3rd Grade: Implications of Piaget's Theory*, Teachers College Press, 1994.

Kawas, Terry. "Contig Jr.," MathWire website, 2009.
mathwire.com/games/contigjr.pdf

Kaye, Peggy. "If you play these games…" from *Games for Math,* Pantheon Books, 1988. If you're homeschooling young children, be sure to check out the other books in Kaye's *Games for…* series.
peggykaye.com

Lockhart, Paul. "Children already know how to learn…" Quoted by Keith Devlin. "Lockhart's Lament—The Sequel," Devlin's Angle, May, 2008.
maa.org/external_archive/devlin/devlin_05_08.html

Péter, Rózsa. "I would like to win over…" from "Mathematics is beautiful," *The Mathematical Intelligencer,* December 1990. Quoted in The MacTutor History of Mathematics archive.
www-history.mcs.st-and.ac.uk/Biographies/Peter.html

Ronda, Erlina R. "Just like the games we play…" from "The Fun in Learning Mathematics Is in the Challenge," Mathematics for Teaching blog, November 12, 2011.
math4teaching.com/fun-in-learning-mathematics-challenge

Rothstein, Edward. "Making Math Magical," *Family Life,* September/October 1996.

Scarne, John, with Clayton Rawson. *Scarne on Dice,* Military Service Publishing Co., 1945.

Trudeau, Richard J. "Mathematics is the world's best game…" from *Dots and Lines,* Kent State University Press, 1976. Updated by Dover Publications as *Introduction to Graph Theory,* 1993.

Weltman, Anna. "Snugglenumber," Recipes for π blog, October 16, 2013.
recipesforpi.wordpress.com/2013/10/16/snugglenumber

Wikipedia Contributors. "Farkle," Wikipedia Internet Encyclopedia.
en.wikipedia.org/wiki/Farkle

—. "Pig (dice game)," Wikipedia Internet Encyclopedia.
en.wikipedia.org/wiki/Pig_%28dice_game%29

Zaslavsky, Claudia. *Tic Tac Toe and Other Three-in-a-Row Games from Ancient Egypt to the Modern Computer,* Thomas Y. Crowell, 1982.

About the Author

Denise Gaskins enjoys math, and she delights in sharing that joy with young people. "Math is not just rules and rote memory," she says. "Math is like ice cream, with more flavors than you can imagine. And if all you ever do is textbook math, that's like eating broccoli-flavored ice cream."

A veteran homeschooling mother of five, Denise has taught or tutored mathematics at every level from pre-K to undergraduate physics. "Which," she explains, "at least in the recitation class I taught, was just one story problem after another. What fun!"

Now she writes the popular Let's Play Math blog and manages the monthly Playful Math Education blog carnival.

A Note from Denise

I hope you enjoyed this book and found new ideas that will help your children enjoy learning. I'd love to connect with you online and to hear your family's experiences with mathematical play.

If you believe this book is worth sharing, please consider posting a review on Goodreads, LibraryThing, or your favorite bookseller's website. An honest review is the highest compliment you can pay to any author, and your comments help fellow readers discover good books.

Thank you!

—Denise Gaskins

Let's connect online: DeniseGaskins.com, LetsPlayMath@gmail.com

Books by Denise Gaskins

tabletopacademy.net/playful-math-books

"Denise has gathered up a treasure trove of living math resources for busy parents. If you've ever struggled to see how to make math come alive beyond your math curriculum (or if you've ever considered teaching math without a curriculum), you'll want to check out this book."
—Kate Snow, author of Multiplication Facts That Stick

Let's Play Math:
How Families Can Learn Math Together—and Enjoy It

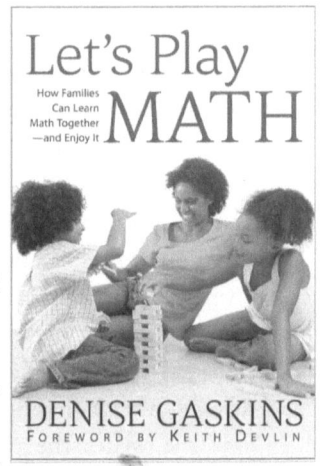

Transform your child's experience of math!

Even if you struggled with mathematics in school, you can help your children enjoy learning and prepare them for academic success.

Author Denise Gaskins makes it easy with this mixture of math games, low-prep project ideas, and inspiring coffee-chat advice from a veteran homeschooling mother of five. Drawing on more than thirty years' teaching experience, Gaskins provides helpful tips for parents with kids from preschool to high school, whether your children learn at home or attend a traditional classroom.

Don't let your children suffer from the epidemic of math anxiety. Pick up a copy of *Let's Play Math*, and start enjoying math today.

Want to help your kids learn math? Claim your free copy of Denise's 24-page problem-solving booklet, and sign up to hear about new books, revisions, and sales or other promotions.

TabletopAcademy.net/Subscribe

The *Math You Can Play* Series

You'll love these math games because they give your child a strong foundation for mathematical success.

By playing these games, you strengthen your child's intuitive understanding of numbers and build problem-solving strategies. Mastering a math game can be hard work. But kids do it willingly because it's fun.

Math games prevent math anxiety. Games pump up your child's mental muscles, reduce the fear of failure, and generate a positive attitude toward mathematics.

So what are you waiting for? Clear off a table, grab a deck of cards, and let's play some math.

Under Construction: The *Playful Math Singles* Series

The Playful Math Singles from Tabletop Academy Press are short, topical books featuring clear explanations and ready-to-play activities.

Word Problems from Literature features story problems for elementary and middle school students based on family-favorite books such as *Mr. Popper's Penguins* and *The Hobbit*. Step by step solutions demonstrate how bar model diagrams can help children reason their way to the answer.

70+ Things To Do with a Hundred Chart shows you how to take your child on a mathematical adventure through playful, practical activities. Who knew math could be so much fun?

More titles coming soon. Watch for them at your favorite online bookstore.

www.ingramcontent.com/pod-product-compliance
Lightning Source LLC
Chambersburg PA
CBHW021123080526
44587CB00010B/615